Summary of Educated: A

Memoir

By

Tara Westover

SpeedyReads

Note to readers:

This is a SpeedyReads guide to Tara Westover's "Educated: A Memoir" meant to enhance your reading experience. You are encouraged to buy the original book.

Claim Your Free Gift Now

As a way of saying "thank you" for your purchase, we're offering you a free special report that's *exclusive* for our book readers.

In **"Delicious Reading: How to Quadruple and Enhance Your Book Reading Experience Within 24 Hours"**, you'll discover simple but powerful ways to heighten and enhance your book reading experience that was only known by the top book connoisseurs…. Until now…

Go to the link below before it expires!

http://www.easysummaries.com/gift

Summary of Educated: A Memoir

Contents

Claim Your Free Gift Now

Summary of Educated: A Memoir

The author, Tara Westover, and her siblings did not go to school, four of them did not have birth certificates and they did not have medical and school records. They only knew mountain life in Idaho.

Summary of Educated: Chapter 1

Tara's father's family had been living at Buck Peak's base for 50 years. Her dad always recited the Bible to them. Her paternal grandmother lived down the hill and her maternal grandmother lived fifteen miles south. Her dad and paternal grandmother argued all the time. Tara's dad considered milk to be linked with the devil and banned it from entering their place, so she started going to her paternal grandma's to have milk. Her paternal grandparents went away in winter since her grandpa is too old for Idaho's winters. Encouraged by her grandma, Tara plans to run away from home with them without letting her parents know.

Summary of Educated: Chapter 2

Tara's dad suggested that her mother should assist the local midwife as one of the ways to be self-reliant. The first case Mother handled was a difficult one since there was a lot of damage and the umbilical cord wrapped around the baby's neck. It was OK in the end but it shook her mother, who was not as open to midwifery as Judy, the midwife. She assisted Judy with some more cases since Dad and many other people did not believe in hospitals. Mother did not want to continue to be a midwife but she had to take it up all on her own when Judy's family moved elsewhere. However, she slowly became accustomed to it after Judy left and even started doing it like Judy.

Her midwifery also changed their lives. She started taking them to restaurants, bought equipment to be a better midwife and also bought a phone. Luke wanted a birth certificate when he was 15 and Mother thought she would get them made for all of them. Tara's case was the hardest since they remembered different birth dates for her. Tara finally received a Delayed Certificate of Birth at age 9. She went with her mother to attend a birth but did not like it.

Summary of Educated: Chapter 3

Tara's parents were Gene and Faye. Faye's mother was overly concerned about propriety and appearances but Faye did not want it. Gene appeared to be serious and naughty at the same time. Tara's paternal grandfather was short-tempered and her grandmother worked very hard. Dad always had the view that a woman's real place is home. As a child, he ran the farm but was still full of energy and laughs when he meets their mother. Gene and Faye met in town where she was serving as a waitress. He was more serious than other guys in his age and different somehow. Tara's maternal uncle Lynn disapproved of the way her father and those around him were when Faye first took him home to meet her family. Tara and her siblings guessed that their maternal family did not approve of the engagement. As a child, Tara did not know much about their mother's family and their father seldom went to their maternal grandmother's house.

The only exception was their aunt Angie, Faye's younger sister, who still wanted to see Faye. In their wedding picture, Gene and Faye were both extremely happy. In the picture, Gene was completely different from the anxious man he's now, gathering food and ammunition to help when the difficult times arrive in the form of the government persecuting them. Tara's oldest brother is Tony, then comes Shawn, then Tyler and further Luke. Then came Audrey, Richard and Tara. Most of them were delivered at home with the assistance of midwives. Gene kept changing with time and made his sons leave school. Then he stopped renewing and registering stuff and started stockpiling food. Tara realized later that he had mental illness that was never diagnosed or treated. Maternal grandma died 3 years ago and Tara searched her face for a lot of things when she did.

Summary of Educated: Chapter 4

During their trip to Arizona, Tyler, 17, slept on the wheel and their station wagon had an accident. They traveled to the mobile home of their paternal grandparents, who were waiting in the desert for the winter to pass. Since their grandma was consulting a doctor, their dad lost his cool and accused her of being an Illuminati agent. Their dad became so unbearable that their mother started leaving the room whenever he entered it. They began their journey one night and met an accident. Faye suffered a serious brain injury and could not even recognize her children properly again. However, they did not go to a hospital. Tyler blamed himself for the accident and everything after that. Tara did not blame anyone and contemplated it in a greater context, with life as its background.

Summary of Educated: Chapter 5

One month after the accident, Tyler announced that he was leaving to go to college. Tony and Shawn had already left by then for different reasons. Tyler, with his speech obstacles, had always been different. He was the different one. He liked books and serenity. While his brothers wrestled, he found solace in music. Tara also started listening to music with him.

During their childhood, their mother believed in homeschooling them while their dad was inclined toward practical skills. Luke was the hardest to learn since he had a learning disability. As time passed, their mother's enthusiasm subsided and a policy of the children learning whatever they wanted to became adopted. Tara was among the least disciplined of the siblings and by the time she was 10, she had only learned the Morse code since her dad insisted. Tara doesn't use to wash her hands after using the toilet even though her maternal grandma disapproved.

In 8th grade, Tyler managed to enroll and stay in school. This instilled in him a thirst for learning and despite unfavorable circumstances, he kept learning. Even though Dad stayed in denial for some time after Tyler's college announcement, Tyler left to step into a world he knew nothing about.

Summary of Educated: Chapter 6

Sometime after Tyler left, Audrey turned 15 and got a driver's license. She also took up jobs and became independent. The family started changing. Owing to the eldest three sons having left, Dad could not build hay sheds anymore and had to confine himself to scrapping. Luke had to play the major supporting role. Richard and Tara acquired his earlier role as grunts. The environment of the junkyard was hostile and like her brothers and others before her, Tara also got injured because of her dad throwing stuff around. By this time, mother had gotten better. Her headaches became less frequent and she started confining herself to the basement.

She resumed her role as a midwife again but had to be supervised. However, mother came back by first mixing oils for different healing purposes, then adopting the habit of muscle testing and further starting energy work. Healing became a spiritual process for her.

Tyler planted the seed of curiosity in Tara and she became interested in studying. Richard also studied encyclopedias in his free time. Tara also read the Book of Mormon and other scriptures. After she hurt herself badly while working, she told her dad that she wanted to go to school. Dad's immediate reaction was to tell her that their family obeys the Lord's commandments. He further referred to the story of Jacob and Esau, which meant that she had

failed to act like the daughter he had raised.

Summary of Educated: Chapter 7

The following summer was rainless. Luke and Richard worked with Dad. One particular lunch was a lot of fun, with Dad cracking jokes throughout. Tara was just 10 at the time and mother was away. Luke's trouser got soaked in gasoline which eventually caught fire while at work. Tara, Richard and Luke's memories share different accounts of what happened next. It is true that Tara treated Luke and Dad returned to the site to stop the fire from spreading. Luke was in a lot of pain and his leg lost a lot of flesh and skin. Despite being against hospital drugs because of the teachings of their dad, Tara wanted to give him morphine but he refused.

Mother then treated the leg further when she returned.

Summary of Educated: Chapter 8

Audrey managed to move away from home by finding a job and Tara, 11, knew that if she wanted to follow suit, she would also have to find a job. She asked Myrna, gas station owner, whether she could put up a notice. Myrna told her that her daughter was looking for someone to babysit her youngest. Tara started babysitting her daughter, Mary's daughter, then her friend, Eve's children. Then she started packing cashews for a guy. She also joined Mary's sister Caroline's dance class in tomboyish clothes, where other girls wore leotards with tights. Tara found the dress immodest but Caroline convinced her mother to buy her those. Tara decided to hide the costume from her Dad.

When Mother didn't agree to the Christmas costume design, Caroline designed sweatshirts for Tara's class. Dad attended the recital and Tata was so scared of his presence that she couldn't perform properly. He shouted on their way back as to how mother could have let her sin so openly. Dad thought the class was Satan's work and the girls moved like whores in the church. Mother, who had allowed it earlier, was convinced by him.

Guilty, mother arranged for Tara to join a choir. When Tara sang at the church and everyone loved it, Dad proudly collected the compliments.

When Dad heard her practicing, he also allowed her to audition for the play *Annie* in town.

Summary of Educated: Chapter 9

Tara sang for *Annie* in 1999. Dad's paranoia about the Days of Abomination was at its peak. He dreaded Y2K and feared everything was going to come to a halt since the government had wrongly programmed the digit calendars. He warned everyone and advised them to store food. However, they continued to lead their lives the normal way. Tara's family prepared and stored food in a root cellar.

Tara had rehearsals at the Worm Creek Opera House and that gave her the first chance to interact with people who went to school and consulted doctors. When Tara needed pretty dresses for her play, her mother took her to Aunt Angie's and she gave them her daughter's beautiful dresses. Dad did not stop Tara from auditioning for more plays. When Tara's tonsils grew bigger, he suggested she stand with her mouth open in the sun. She did it for a month but it did not help much.

She met Charles at Worm Creek and he told her that her singing was the best he had ever heard. With Christmas approaching, Dad's anticipation of Y2K reached its peak. When nothing happened on the night of 31st December, Dad sat in front of the TV for long, waiting for something to happen, and was disappointed when nothing did.

Summary of Educated: Chapter 10

With the year 2000 unfolding like any other, Dad's spirits dampened. Mother announced the need for another Arizona trip. With Luke busy, only the parents, Richard, Audrey and Tara went. The Arizona sun, like always, breathed a new life into Dad. Grandma had a lot of doctor visits owing to bone marrow cancer. Tired of chemotherapy and all, grandma asked Mother for her herbs. Dad thought that wouldn't work since grandma had betrayed her faith by consulting doctors.

On their way back, the weather changed to icy winter and Dad took the wheel from Richard. They had an accident again and an ambulance and cops arrived. Dad had to call Rob and Diane Hardy when he could not reach his sons. Sometime after the accident, Tara could not move her neck. It became so severe that Tara could not stand without holding something for support. Her mother called an energy specialist but it did not help. Tara was in bed for a month and couldn't move her neck. Shawn visited them and told her she needed a chiropractor. He helped her and she could move her neck. She started viewing him as a defender of some sort.

Summary of Educated: Chapter 11

Their paternal grandpa abandoned ranching and farming with age. He used to auction wild horses every year. For that reason, Tara and Shawn tamed some horses. Tara took the saddle with a horse named Bud.

Shawn wanted to bid adieu to his old life and started spending more and more time at home. He also started dropping Tara off to her lessons. One day, when Tara was riding Bud and Shawn was riding a newly saddled mare, Tara got too close to the mare. The mare became hysterical, which caused hysteria in Bud. Both Tara and Shawn somehow managed to control their horses and Shawn took charge of Bud in the end.

Summary of Educated: Chapter 12

When Tony's wife got sick and the doctor suggested bed rest, Tony asked Shawn if he could take charge of his rig for some time. Shawn took Tara along. They went trucking to Las Vegas and other places such as Washington State. The trip was a lot of fun. A girl who came to the Opera House with Charles, Sadie, started coming to the junkyard for Shawn. Shawn told Tara that Sadie has fish eyes i.e. she's stupid. But it made him jealous to see her with Charles. He once told her she has lovely eyes like a fish.

Sadie's parents were divorced. Shawn became interested in her but got jealous when he saw her with Charles. To punish her, he stopped talking to her. She got desperate and asked the boys at high school not to talk to her. Shawn punished her severely by asking for things repeatedly that she would fetch. Once Shawn got back, Tara spilled water over him in retaliation and Shawn punished her brutally in the bathroom. The problem was that it did not affect Tara like she expected it to be.

Summary of Educated: Chapter 13

When the twin towers fell, that was the very first time Tara heard of them. Three days later, Audrey, 19, got married to Benjamin, whom she met while waitressing. Dad predicted that war would take away his sons. Tara forgave Shawn for the night in the bathroom the night of the wedding since she feared the future war.

Tara's body was changing and she did not want to remain a child. Her dad was criticizing some women for dressing, bending etc. the wrong way and it stayed with her for a long time, questioning the way she was doing things and thinking she was growing up to be the wrong kind of woman.

When Tara started wearing makeup, Shawn criticized her. Charles told Tara he was in love with Sadie and Shawn criticized Tara for talking to Charles. Sadie and Shawn broke up and Shawn started going out with an old girlfriend. When Sadie accepted Charles's date, it made Shawn angry. When he was being violent to Tara for being a slut like others, Tyler arrived and saved her.

However, Tara later asked Shawn to stop her from becoming a woman like others. He promised he would. Tyler asked her to go to school and told her BYU takes homeschoolers. Tara changed her bedroom door locks.

Summary of Educated: Chapter 14

Dad got a contract and Shawn and others got busy. Randy, Tara's boss, taught her how to use the internet. Tyler asked Tara to buy books to prepare for the ACT exam. Even though Tara was not interested in college, Tyler convinced her by telling her about studying music. She checked BYU's website and bought an ACT study guide. Even when mother couldn't help her with algebra, she bought a huge algebra textbook. She learned a lot but when she couldn't understand trigonometry and even mother failed to explain it, she asked Dad. She later learned it from Tyler.

Shawn fell at work one day and experienced a serious internal brain injury. Tara left work and became his attendant, which gave her a chance to learn trigonometry in peace as well. Sadie also started visiting. Doctors told mother that Shawn's personality transformed due to the incident and he might always be unpredictable and violent. Tara convinced herself that he had never been cruel before and the accident made him so.

Summary of Educated: Chapter 15

Dad visited Tara in her room and told her about God's wrath concerning her decision to go to college. When she told mother she would not go to BYU, mother told her she was the one she always expected to go and told her she should. Without Shawn's help, Dad's construction business suffered. When he went back to scrapping, Tara also did since she needed the money. The ACT scared her since so many wanted to go to BYU.

After taking the exam, Tara thought that she had failed in math and was sure that she had indeed failed science. Having seen her fellow students, she found it funny that she thought she might reach the top 15%.

On a hot day, if Tara rolled her sleeves to let an inch of her shoulders visible, Dad would unrolled them and she too would kept rerolling it since it was so hot. Tara's test results showed a 22. It wasn't 27 that she required for BYU but it still promised a door to possibilities. Tara was 16 then.

Shawn returned to work. After the Shear, a deadly machine Dad brought, injured Luke's arm, Dad asked Tara to work it. She obliged. Shawn arrived and objected and it led to a brawl between Shawn and Dad. Dad did not let go. Shawn and Tara worked the Shear together for a month.

Summary of Educated: Chapter 16

When construction started on the milking barn in Oneida, Shawn wanted Tara to drive the crane. Dad protested but they went ahead. Whenever Dad got angry, Shawn was the only one who could stand up to him and walk away.

Anytime Tara is studying to retake her ACT, Shawn would come and both would watch movie together. He assured her of her smartness and that she would get her 27. Shawn went back on his motorbike and Tara after some time in her car. Shawn met an accident and had a hole in his head in such a manner that Tara could see his brain. When she called home, Dad wanted her to bring Shawn home but she was encouraged by the people who gathered at the scene, to take him to the hospital. The doctor said the damage was minimal and stitched the hole. They went home. Tara was ashamed of being a traitor since she went to the hospital. Tara got 28 in her second attempt at the ACT and got admission in BYU. Dad threw a huge tantrum sometime after that, when Tara and Mother returned from their apartment hunt. With Christmas approaching, Tara feared something terrible was going to happen. Tyler was getting married.

Summary of Educated: Chapter 17

Mother drove Tara to her apartment in city on New Year's Day. When Tara met her first housemate Shannon, she was immensely disappointed by her immodest dressing. When she met Mary, the second housemate, dressed for church, she was relieved but was disappointed again when Mary went grocery shopping on a Sunday i.e. on Sabbath, since it was a sin in Tara's household.

Classes started. Tara felt even more loyal to Dad despite her ignorance but when she asked her professor about what Holocaust meant, he told her not to joke and when her classmate Vanessa told her the same thing, she read up on Holocaust and was ashamed of her ignorance. After church, her housemates wanted to see a movie but she refused since she doesn't watch movies on Sunday. Even after filing for Sunday school, Tara thought she had disobeyed the Lord.

Summary of Educated: Chapter 18

Tara did not believe in cleaning the apartment much even if there was rotten stuff in the fridge. She wasn't used to washing her hands after using the toilet. The atmosphere in the apartment was tense. Tara failed her western civilization exam. She didn't want to tell her family. She called home and told her father it was more difficult than she had expected. He said it would be OK, and he told her he would help with the money and asked her to come home for comfort. She was really touched. Before the next western civilization exam, Vanessa and Tara studied together and Vanessa asked her to read the textbook, which astonished Tara. She followed the advice and got a B. By the end of the semester, she started getting A's. The professor discarded the first exam later and Tara's first failure did not matter anymore.

Summary of Educated: Chapter 19

At the end of the semester, Tara came back to Buck's Peak. The grades were to be disclosed some time later and would determine her fate. She needed money and got herself a job at Stokes back. When she went home, Dad told her she would be working for him that summer. She declined since it would mean going backward. Dad was not ready to let go. She called Tyler. Tyler asked her what she wanted him to do. He must have meant it literally but she thought otherwise and cut the call. She quit her job at Stokes and started crapping for her dad. Shawn had changed by then and seemed quite serene. He was studying for his GED and told her he wanted to study law.

Shawn and Tara went to the Opera House. Charles met them there and asked her to a movie. The movie was vulgar and she did not like it. He called her after it and they talked for a long time. He made plans to get a burger on Friday night. Tara bought girly jeans and two shirts and when she wore those clothes on her date with Charles, she felt really different. They had a great time and started spending time together a lot. Tara passed with A's in every subject except Western Civ. promised a half scholarship. When Charles touched her hand for the first time, she jerked it away. Her father's words haunted her.

Summary of Educated: Chapter 20

Dad thought she was becoming 'uppity' and made work more difficult for her to remind her of her roots. Shawn agreed with him and they became comrades. Shawn called her 'nigger' when she blackened her face earlier at work but now that she had learned its history and connotations, she hated it and understood the ignorance of her family.

Summary of Educated: Chapter 21

Tara knew that her father wouldn't be able to pay for her BYU semester fees and he truly didn't do so. The headache she felt on her last day at home prevented her from going to church but Charles did take her to his home and gave her medicine. She took the medicine with great trepidation. She took her father's recently bought car to university in return for his lack of complete help in paying tuition. Once back to the campus, she shifted into an apartment with Robin, Megan and Jenni. Her algebra course reduced her to a stressful mess and it wasn't till she talked to the professor that she gained some control over herself. Tara planned to study algebra

on Thanksgiving.

Summary of Educated: Chapter 22

Thanksgiving would have been good if it had not been for Shawn's presence. Shawn teased her into shouting and the result was a physically violent reaction that shook Charles to his core enough that he told her that she must work for herself too, to get better. With a broken toe in her foot, she returned to her university where through her hard work, she pulled an 'A' grade. Return to home for Christmas was another troubling event. Her dad was confident that Richard would clear his ACT while Richard didn't feel that way about the ACT. Shawn assaulted her again outside a public location, where he knew Charles might be present. However, Tara continued to laugh and act as if nothing was wrong with her when in reality her ankle and arm had been hurt. Her accounts in her journals finally turned negative towards Shawn.

Summary of Educated: Chapter 23

Tara started running low on cash and it was then she realized that she wouldn't be able to make it to the next semester. She even sold her horse. Robin, on the other hand, was concerned about her and her multiplying pain. Toothache became her worst enemy. Shawn showed a rare moment of kindness by giving her $100. Robin made her see the Bishop with regards to her situation and the Bishop helped her realize the role of everyone at her home to her discontent. It was ultimately the Bishop and her friend Robin who pushed her to get the money from the government i.e. a grant, something that her parents had warned her against but due to their insistence she became brave enough to get the required documents from home and get the grant money. She finally had her course books and got her tooth treated. She was going to continue at the university.

Summary of Educated: Chapter 24

Money was a new thing for her. A stable account led her to use her mind to worry about other things than the money issue. For the first time in forever, she started taking a keen interest in her studies and it was during her psychology lecture that she realized that her father probably had bipolar disorder. This made her choose this topic for her class project. She learned that her father could have been treated and chose not to do so. Her coming back home resulted into shouting at her father for his lack of treatment. She returned to her university and shifted from her area to another. At the new church, she met Nick, who learned to care for her.

She was made to visit a doctor for her throat concerns. One day, Audrey called to tell her that her father had been in an accident and that she should hurry back home.

Summary of Educated: Chapter 25

She remembered that her childhood had been filled with stories of how her grandfather was once riding on his mare one day, out in the mountain, when suddenly his horse was scared by the presence of a snake and threw him off into the rocks. The rocks caused injury and as a result of the impact, he fainted. When he woke up, he was in his home's front porch. This was attributed to an angel's existence. How her own father similarly managed to get away from the burning location to her mother's house, in his burned condition, would always remain a mystery to her. Her father resisted medical treatment and so, her mother referred to her own herbal concoctions. The burns were extreme and Tara thought that her father might die anytime. However, he lived through the worst of it.

Summary of Educated: Chapter 26

Shawn soon announced his engagement with a teenager named Emily and Tara started fearing for her. It was her fear that made her go out on a long horse ride and camping trip with Emily and Shawn. Tara's father started learning about the things going on in her life since he was listening to others for the first time in his life, due to his damaged oral cavity. She returned to the university and realized that there was a growing chasm between her and Nick. She wanted to tell Nick about everything and yet couldn't do so. After Emily and Shawn's wedding in September, she broke up with Nick because she couldn't feel the connection.

Summary of Educated: Chapter 27

Tara started getting her interest changed and was no longer attracted to the study of music. She began inclined toward masculine interests and this was what drove her to study politics, history and geography. A peer's sexist remark made her go to her professor in order to gain a perspective on how she should get back to her feminine ideals. However, the professor told her about a Cambridge university program and she applied for it. Emily got pregnant and her pregnancy became erratic. Her labor started early and it was Tara's mother's medicine that kept her from giving birth. Her father and mother turned the whole horrid episode of burns and blasts into a spiritual experience. Tara had a lot of trouble in getting a passport after getting into the program but finally, she did get her passport. Emily gave birth prematurely to Peter, a child doomed to have several surgeries and pulmonary disabilities.

Summary of Educated: Chapter 28

Soon, Tara was in Cambridge along with the other selected few who were lucky enough to be a part of the course. Dr. Kerry took them all to the ancient cathedral's roof and that was where he discovered that Tara could be comfortable too in her selected surroundings. Tara's supervisor turned out to be the celebrated Professor Steinberg, a great historian of the Holocaust, among other things. When he learned about Tara's educational upbringing, he called the event Shaw's Pygmalion. Her supervisor took great interest in her works and in her mind's working, and in response to one of her works, he told her that she would be able to go to any university she desired because she had a great mind. Tara remained intimidated with the glamour of the location and felt that she wasn't a part of the scenery.

Summary of Educated: Chapter 29

Tara applied for Gates scholarship after being pressured by Professor Steinberg and never considered that she might get in. Eventually she got in and cleared her interview later. Her parents visited her one night out of the blue and she took them out. It was during one of her conversations with them that she realized that her father's assumptions now held no power over her mind in the new atmosphere. She considered that the influence might have been the effect of the hill side where her parents were bigger than life for her. A fellow questioned her on the Mormon traditions of polygamy and she couldn't answer that she disliked the concept of polygamy just like him. Over a dispute with her father, her parents failed to show up at her graduation event until quite late. It was her parents who later dropped her off at the airport for her trip to a foreign land.

Summary of Educated: Chapter 30

Cambridge, Trinity College was amazing in all its glory. Tara realized soon that the students of the college were far beyond her level of knowledge. The material studied in classes had some basics regarding the independence of mind and physical world that she couldn't grasp because she had never felt them. Tara later realized her ignorance of the most basic content on feminism and devoted day and night to learn about the revolutions. She finally learned that there was no definition of a woman and she could be anyone at all and still be a woman. It was on Christmas that she returned to Idaho, while Richard and his new family showed her a contrast of the old and new worlds. It was Emily's haggard appearance that showed her that the deterioration of women in her family continued.

Summary of Educated: Chapter 31

Before she went back to England, she took it upon herself to visit Audrey at her place. Tara realized that Audrey's life might have been hers if she hadn't stepped up to get an education. Later, Audrey discovered that Tara was also bullied by their brother Shawn and at this point, Tara realized that her sister might also have suffered at their brother's hand. On her return to the university, she immersed herself in her studies and after her final exams, she went to Rome with a group of friends. Rome might have triggered her inner fanatic had she not been exposed to her peer's intelligent discourse about the place, history and philosophy. On her return to campus, she learned that her sister told their mother and her mother finally apologized for her behavior. Tara felt relieved for the first time in her life.

Summary of Educated: Chapter 32

The impending death of her paternal grandma brought Tara back to Idaho. Drew took that as an opportunity to spend some time with Tara. However, Tara was concerned that he would consider her parents abnormal if he were to hear their theories and took him out in the mountains. On her return home, she found the house quiet and discovered that her grandma had passed away. The whole house turned quiet and her father, who had turned into a lively man, retreated to his old mannerisms. After the funeral, Tara heard her father telling her mother to do 'wifely' duties of handling home and relations. Tara's mother stood up for herself for the first time, and Tara's dad was left cooking his own meals.

Summary of Educated: Chapter 33

Her return to Cambridge was consumed with guilt over leaving behind her sister alone in the harsh environment back in Idaho, while her sister had tried to get support from her over the issue with Shawn. Tara had told her that their mother would help her through. Drew came to Cambridge for his Master's degree and Tara's life became busier by the day. The possibility that she might get into the PhD program at the university drove Tara to excellence. Her topic centered on the Mormon movement from a social perspective. She soon returned to Idaho for Christmas where the situation between her parents had calmed down. She met Luke and Shawn. Shawn deceived her once again into thinking that she was safe from him. Later Shawn cursed Audrey's existence for the 'lies' she was spewing. Tara remained safe because she didn't confess her involvement in the issue.

Summary of Educated: Chapter 33

Her return to Cambridge was consumed with guilt over leaving behind her sister alone in the harsh environment back in Idaho, while her sister had tried to get support from her over the issue with Shawn. Tara had told her that their mother would help her through. Drew came to Cambridge for his Master's degree and Tara's life became busier by the day. The possibility that she might get into the PhD program at the university drove Tara to excellence. Her topic centered on the Mormon movement from a social perspective. She soon returned to Idaho for Christmas where the situation between her parents had calmed down. She met Luke and Shawn. Shawn deceived her once again into thinking that she was safe from him. Later Shawn cursed Audrey's existence for the 'lies' she was spewing. Tara remained safe because she didn't confess her involvement in the issue.

Summary of Educated: Chapter 34

On her return home, she went up to Dad to talk to him about the threats Shawn was making towards Audrey. It turned out that her father didn't believe her story one bit and desired proofs for each and every act of violence that she thought her brother had committed. She was left speechless. Later, Dad invited Shawn home to stand up for him and this drove Tara over the edge. Tara lied to make the consequences of such confessions go away but Shawn managed to scare her by passing her a blade that still had blood on it. The next day, Tara made a run for Salt Lake City. On her way, she saw Shawn's trailer and the pooled blood, the blood of Diego, a pure bred dog. Tara knew then that Shawn's rage

had been transferred to the poor animal.

Summary of Educated: Chapter 35

Tara spent the rest of her holidays with Drew in Salt Lake City and later went back to Cambridge. She considered that it wouldn't be long before Shawn realized that she had lied that day in Idaho and soon, his emails and telephone calls caught her. He threatened to kill her himself or send an assassin to do so. She called her parents to inform them about her brother's delusional statements and her parents denied the behavior. She won a summer grant to study in Paris and moved there with Drew. The denial of her sister Audrey came days later where her sister told her that she had confessed to their father that it was Tara's influence that drove her to state such things. To feel like herself, she started denying the existence of the truth till Shawn's ex-girlfriends also confessed to similar mistreatments.

Summary of Educated: Chapter 36

September saw Tara enter into Harvard University and she immersed herself in different forms of coursework. She had let go of her expectations with her family. They were not going to accept her and she busied herself with her books. However, a surprise came in the form of her parents' visit to Harvard and she realized that they were there for her atonement. They took her to the temple and yet Tara couldn't feel any change after a visit to the holy place. Her father offered to give her his blessings so that the devil may leave her but she declined because now she had learned to value her intellect above her father's stubbornness. Her denial

made her parents retreat from her.

Summary of Educated: Chapter 37

Sleepwalking and anxiety became Tara's best friends in the following days and she started losing all her academic interests in the university to the point where her PhD was threatened. She returned home to get her peace back, to get her parents to bless her mind. Once back, she needed to write an email to Drew and when she turned on her mother's computer, she read the interactions between her mother and Shawn's ex-girlfriend. She discovered that her mother was a shadow of her father, presenting her fanatic thoughts on Tara to everyone who would listen. Tara made a break for it and later got a call from Tyler who sympathized with her but

Tara didn't trust him. She went to the Middle East to meet Drew after her year at the university ended.

Summary of Educated: Chapter 38

She had decided that her brother Tyler would leave her alone just as Audrey had done but it turned out that Tyler was persistent in his stance against their parents. Tara realized that sooner or later, his stance would give way and later found herself with an email that had been carefully drafted by her brother and his wife over the issue of Shawn. Tyler ultimately stood with Tara and against their family. Tara continued to feel guilty and thankful for the act of kindness. Tara finally took help from a counselor and this helped ease her mind with reality. She took back control of her life and her academic career took off. She finally had a thesis topic that was close to her heart i.e. family. After she received her doctorate, she decided to go back home.

Summary of Educated: Chapter 39

Tara thought that her family was lost and yet went back to meet the ones who would accept her. Her grandfather certainly wasn't one of them initially. Tyler and his wife were more than happy to have her while her own mother refused to talk or meet her. Later, she returned to Idaho, living with her estranged Aunt Angie. Tara became close with her mother's family and that was a surprise to her since she thought that her mother's poison would be permanent. Tyler, Richard and Tara continued to be the only ones who remained out of their parent's strongly held beliefs while the rest rotted under their influence, both religious and financial.

Summary of Educated: Chapter 40

Tara has yet to meet her parents and the other siblings that are part of their parents' cult. The changes in Tara were a result of her own choices, choices that educated her. She believes that the distance between her and her father is for the best. The stories from Buck's Peak, Idaho, are best heard from a long distance. She thinks back and considers that it was her repeated assertions to herself about the issues at home that really helped her in healing and moving on. The real change she considered happened when her father decided not to believe in her and when she had to stand up for herself against the odds. Tara doesn't know when she will return to

Idaho but there's hope.

Do you want special deals?

Our mission is to bring you the highest quality companion books on the most popular books on the planet to enrichen and heighten your reading experience like never before!

We frequently give out free books or 0.99 discounted promotions. Be in the loop and receive

special notifications by subscribing to our SpeedyReads membership mailing list. By subscribing, you'll not only receive updates on the latest offer, you'll get "juicy" background information about novels you love, as well as a free copy of **"Delicious Reading: How to Quadruple and Enhance Your Book Reading Experience Within 24 Hours" report and video package.**

Check out:

http://www.easysummaries.com/gift

to sign up to SpeedyReads Free Membership!

FINAL SURPRISE BONUS

Hope you enjoyed this book as much as we enjoyed bring it to you!

I always like to overdeliver, so I'd like to give you one final bonus.

Do me a favor, if you enjoyed this book, please leave a review.   It'll help get the word out so more people can find out more about this wonderful book.

If you do, I'll send you a **FREE SECRET BONUS SECTIONS that didn't make it into this book! (including Trivia Games, Tantalizing Discussion Questions, etc!) (Worth $27)**

Here's what to do:

> 1. Leave a review (longer the better but we'd be grateful whichever length)
> 2. Send your review page URL as well as your username to: speedyreads24@gmail.com
> 3. Receive your bonus within a few hours after we check it!

That's it! Thanks again for purchasing this book and please be sure to check out our other high quality SpeedyReads books!

Warmly,

The SpeedyReadsTeam

Made in the USA
San Bernardino, CA
02 July 2018